T0004232

Celebrate Life

Celebrate Life

JOE COHEN

ETTA DACHMAN

STEVEN GOLD

FLORENCE MENDEL

FLORDELISA MOTA

JORGE RIVERA

ROSE SMEENK

DOROTHY SALVAGE

Copyright © 2008 by Joe Cohen, Etta Dachman, Steven Gold, Florence Mendel,
Flordelisa Mota, Jorge Rivera, Rose Smeenk, Dorothy Salvage.

ISBN: Softcover   978-1-4363-0052-0

All rights reserved. No part of this book may be reproduced or transmitted in any
form or by any means, electronic or mechanical, including photocopying, recording,
or by any information storage and retrieval system, without permission in writing
from the copyright owner.

This book was printed in the United States of America.

To order additional copies of this book, contact:
Xlibris Corporation
1-888-795-4274
www.Xlibris.com
Orders@Xlibris.com
43522

Contents

Joe Cohen

Etta Dachman

Stephen Gold

Florence Mendel

Flordelisa Mota

Jorge Rivera

Rose Smeenk

Dorothy Salvage

Joe Cohen

He was born in Russia; his parents immigrated to the United States, when he was six years old. Mr. Cohen served in World War II for 4 ½ years. That war, and President Franklyn Roosevelt, influenced his thoughts and actions to this day.

A MAN'S BEST FRIEND

Joe Cohen

You have hunting dogs
Tracking dogs
Dogs sniffing for cancer
Seeing eye dogs
Guard dogs.
A man's best friend is a dog
Unlike a human, he will
Forgive and forget.
He will walk with you
At night or any time.
Every one of your moods
He senses.
Take a dog to a hospital ward
And the patients level of
Anxiety will be reduced.
Yes, a dog is a man's
Best friend
Treat him with affection!

MONOLGUE BY GEORGE

(With apologies to Shakespeare)
Joe Cohen

To lie or not to lie? That is the question
Whether it is nobler in the mind
To suffer the slings and arrows of the less fortunate for
Who would bear the whips and the scorns of time
The oppressors wrong, the laws delay
I will never be elected unless
I take up arms against *Iraq,*
And end a sea of trouble
For in time of war, a President
Is never voted out of office
To tell the truth or not to tell the truth?
That is the question
If I do tell this truth
About Iraq funding cuts for education
Who will vote for me?
How will I be remembered?
Oh, to be elected once!
Out, out damn lie
All the words in the dictionary
Can not wipe out this
Stain of lying.
Ah, there is the rub – the dictionary
I'll have my good friend Ashcan
Go into every library;
Check who reads the dictionary,
For terrorists use the book
And make a bonfire with the dictionary
Then publish a new one
Without the word lie in it
Then no one can say "I lie"
Except to say, "I lie me down to sleep."

AT ONE WITH NATURE

Joe Cohen

There is no wrath
like that of a woman scorned.
There is no fury like that
of a volcano that has just erupted
There is no warmth like that
of a woman pleased
or that of the sun
peeking through the clouds.
A Woman's Voice is
Soothing to the ears
Just like a babbling brook
flowing through the years.
A woman in tears
can soften the coldest heart
the drip, drip, of the rain
can make the sidewalk part.
The sun setting and
a woman's curves
both are pleasing to the eyes,
soothing to the nerves.
Treat them gently and
you will be rewarded, "Plentily."

THE REPUBLICANS

Joe Cohen
(The political party was undecided whether to hold
the convention on a cruise ship or at M.S.G.)

The Republicans are coming
The Republicans are coming
Light the lantern in the window
One by land
Two by sea
They are coming to rob you and me
Of our Social Security and precious liberty
And like a thief in the night with lies and distortion
They rob a woman's right to an abortion.
We meet the enemy on top of the Hill
And will not fire till we see the
Lies in their shifty eyes
With Truth Serum as our ammunition we
Will send them to perdition.

COME BACK JESUS

Joe Cohen

Come back Jesus come back
The world needs you
Walk the streets once again
Make the lame walk
And the blind see
Walk into the Temple of the Lord
And chase the money lenders

Come back, Jesus, come back
The warlords are loose again
Killing innocent men women
And children
Taking from the poor and
Giving to the rich

Come back Jesus come back
The world needs you
Make the warlords see again
Heal their souls, so veterans
200,000 don't have to wait
One to two years for healthcare
Because the one who speaks to
Your father
Closed down the Veterans Hospitals

Come back Jesus come back
Come back
Be extra careful when you do
The rich and powerful will
Try to kill you, so be careful.

KATRINA

Joe Cohen

Water, water, everywhere,
But few National Guardsmen in sight
Because the President thought it best
To send them to Iraq to fight
Bodies floating all around
Bobbing up and down
While the President is on his merry-go-round
Looking like a clown and
Still reading my "Pet goat"
And the dead bodies still continue to float.
Katrina, a disaster, will happen once more
Unless the next President will not
Corporations, adore.

LET OUR PEOPLE GROW

Joe Cohen

When our people where
In sweatshop land
Let our people go
They worked so hard
They couldn't stand
Let our people grow
Go down way down
In sweatshop land
Organize
Tell them, to raise the minimum
To a living wage
So "wageslaves" don't
Have to work at two or three jobs
To pay for food and rent
Go down way down
And lift our people up
Or else we'll smite
Your Republican Congress Down
Come election time.

LONELY

Joe Cohen

I'm lonely
Two souls that pass
In the night
Needing love
And friendship.
Neither embracing it
Both too proud
To extend their hand,
And heart, and say
Hello I'm lonely
Aren't you

LOVE

Joe Cohen

You say you love me but do you
I wonder if your love is true
I dress especially for our date
Yet I wait because you are late
Once or twice I can understand
Every "nite" I can't comprehend
What should I do I'm at a loss
Is it because you are cross
I love you dear in every way
Winter and summer night or day
True love is very hard to find
So to me please be very kind
I'm late because I own a store
And am looking to own some more.

MOONLIGHT

Joe Cohen

A man and woman, lovers hugging, kissing and holding hands
Gazing occasionally at the moon lit sky and bright stars

The moon lit sky and bright stars
The man in the moon was saying

"Young lovers, this is your day
Your moment

Don't let it slip by, follow your heart."

They looked at each other, kissed

Went into the parked car
And drove away to heaven.

REMEMBER

Joe Cohen

Do you remember
The first time,
The pleasures, joys
And exhilaration?
I remember – how
Can I forget?
It was my first date.
I picked her up at
Her apartment
She had brown hair
And large hazel eyes
The popular song
"Jeepers creepers"
Was going through
My mind
I took her hand
And we walked to
The subway
With two dollars
And two tickets
In my pocket
I felt like a king
We sat through the
Opera Carmen
When it was over
We came home late.
This was my first
Opera
I shall never
Forget that night.

THE BEGGAR

Joe Cohen

He stands on the street
Not saying a word.
He doesn't have to
His eyes do all the talking
His smiling eyes and
Extended palm
Say everything.
I wonder where he sleeps
Or what and when he eats
Some people, passing by, give him
A dollar – how far does that go?
The beggar – another
Human being who lost his job.
Will you lose your job?

THE DEVIL

Joe Cohen

There is joy in Senior town
As we walk hand in hand
To the Promised Land
Of low cost drugs

Then, walking through the labyrinth of words
Joy turns to bewilderment
Then, anger

As we meet "Co-payments", premiums and deductible.
Will we pay more or less?

The devil is in the details

There is joy in corporate land
No labyrinth for them
Just straight talk,
Subsidies and tax benefits
Like
$139billion
$12 billion
$25 billion
The sky is the limit
And the icing on the cake.
No reimportation of American made drugs

Who said there is no Santa Clause?
The devil is in the White House.

THE LETTER

Joe Cohen

A letter is opened – it's from
The War Department.
Your husband – her tearful eyes
Cannot see any further.
Her sobs make her six month old
Baby cry.
Their dream is dead. He enlisted to get
An education to go to college to
Fulfill the American Dream.
Married two years, a six months old,
He will never see. Never hear the words,
"Daddy I love you", or feel his little arms
Around his neck, lovingly looking into
His face. His dream is dead – but The Army
Did educate him, taught him to hate
Hate someone he never saw and a
Strange name he can't pronounce
Taught him to kill. To kill someone else's
Dream.
The Army, teaches very well, those from
the wrong side of the track.
When will they stop teaching?
When will the letters stop coming?

TO BE FREE

Joe Cohen

Freedom is a road
One must travel on
A road that never ends
The American slaves
Traveled that road,
Ran away, revolted and
Finally achieved their goal,
At the end of the Civil War.
But without those
"40 acres and a mule,"
They were forced to "Rent themselves"
Out to their former masters.
They were forced to travel once more
On the freedom road, and
They met Martin Luther King, Jr.
Who led them to a
Higher stage of freedom.
He cleared the path of the
Many obstacles, the slavocracy
Put in their way, and finally
They won the same rights
As a White man.
Now, how free are we?
White, Brown, Black, Yellow.
Truly, we cannot be free
Without a good college education
Without a good paying occupation
And a roof over our heads
That road and struggle
Is a continuing one.
Once again we have to
Put our walking shoes on –
That road never ends.

TRUTH IS COMING TO TOWN

Joe Cohen

You better not lie
You better not spy
You better not pry
I'm telling you why
Truth is coming to town
You better not try
To pull the wool over our eyes
I'm telling you why
Truth is coming to town
He is making a list of
Your double talk
And your dirty tricks.
Truth is coming to town
Mothers and Fathers are crying
Because their sons and daughters
Are now dying,
While you are denying
That you were lying.
Truth is coming to town
You are lying when you're sleeping
And lying when you are awake
We hope to impeach you
For our country's sake –
Truth is coming to town.

TWILIGHT YEARS

Joe Cohen

As we reach the
Twilight of our lives
Growing older gracefully
Singing, dancing, and
Making merry
Living like there is
No tomorrow
A cold clammy voice
Interrupts our dancing.
"The Social Security floor
Can not support
The present dancers, and
All the future dancers.
The floor will collapse.
To save the Social Security
Floor, we will remove
Some of the planks"
A warm mature voice replies:
"Why are you scaring us, the
Social Security floor
Will last till 2052,
So buzz off and
Let us dance."

WAR

Joe Cohen

War is not good
for flowers and little children,
birds, bees, and even the trees.
Nature abhors the horror of wars.
Where truth is left behind under
the weight and grind of lies, lies, and more lies.
Let us have peace. It is good for motherhood, fatherhood,
brotherhood, flowers and little children.

WHY

Joe Cohen

Powder puffs floating in the sky.
A lantern hanging nearby.
People looking up and
Wondering why.
Why life, why death?
Is life death? Is death life?
It's all a mystery to me.
Will it ever be otherwise?

Etta Dachman

Was born in New York City of parents who came from Russia. She graduated from Hunter College and worked as an accountant for a short time. She married and had two children, decided to change careers and become a teacher. She worked for twenty-eighth years in the Bronx, District 10, and retired seventeen years ago. Her hobbies included travel, oil painting and the recorder. She attends three Senior Centers for varied activities. This is her first experience in writing poetry.

CROWDS

Etta Dachman

The bus was very crowded
Like a can of packed sardines.
There was not a space there
Of which I was aware.
"Move to the back," shouted the driver
He was getting impatient and madder.
Some people had heavy packages
Mothers carried babies and carriages.
A few people started to grumble
There wasn't any sign of trouble.
I was sitting in front of the bus
I was able to get off without a fuss.

DANIELLE

Etta Dachman

When I think of her
I hear beautiful singing
Sweeter than my ears
Have ever heard.

When I see her
I love her beautiful smile.
Inside there is much goodness
To love her more.

I touch her hair
Which is curly down to her shoulders.
No artist can portray
Or frame her face.

I call her the "Princess"
Because of her youthfulness.
Danielle is bright
I think she is such a delight.

FALL

Etta Dachman

After summer, comes fall
This is the season of football.
The days are getting shorter
The nights are a little longer
The weather is cooler.
The leaves are turning brown
And are beginning to fall down.
Children are back in school
To learn the golden rule
There is reading, writing and arithmetic
And other subjects that are basic.
Apples are in season
To eat them is a good reason
There are apple cider, apple pie, and apples on a stick
Also apples that one can pick.
The sights, sounds, and smells of fall
Are delightful to us all.

FLOW

Etta Dachman

When a river flows south
It deposits silt in its mouth.
When water flows in a heavy rain
It usually floods the plain.
When blood flows in an artery or vein
It ends up in the brain
Then the flow of ideas is born.
Policemen regulate the flow of traffic
Otherwise, it would be very chaotic.

HATS

Etta Dachman

In winter, I wear hats
Hats can be worn in all seasons
For many different reasons.
In summer hats are worn in the sun
And at parties just for fun.
A Mexican may wear a sombrero
In Spain men wear hats dancing a bolero.
A king and queen may wear a crown
There is a hat for a circus clown.
A chef, in his hat, prepares the main course
A cowboy is active in a rodeo on a horse.
Many workers wear hats, while in action
As well as for protection.
There are many customs about hats worldwide
Also for different religious designes.

IRAQ

Etta Dachman

There is much news on Iraq and war
All this is happening without a rule of law
Sunni fighting Shiite
All day and sometimes night
Mortar attacks in a neighborhood
Torture of hundreds which is not good
It doesn't seem like we're accomplishing things there
We are spending so much money, everywhere
Many Americans have died
Wounded soldiers have multiplied.
The President says, "We cannot abandon them now."
We have to send more troops, anyhow.

LOVE

Etta Dachman

Love is a powerful emotion
Full of respect and devotion.
Love grows slowly
You don't notice it at first
It adds a little bit to itself everyday.
A union of two lovers is
Learning about each other
Sharing many activities.
Infatuation, at first, may set in
In the end, it doesn't win.
Infatuation fades away
Love is here to stay.

RED

Etta Dachman

Red is a color I like to wear
It goes well with my skin and my hair.
They say that red is becoming to me
Whether it is a coat, dress, or a tee.
The color is warm and exciting
Red in my living room is inviting.
Whenever I am able
I have red flowers on my table.
Red flowers, I used to paint
On my walls, they look so quaint.

RETIREMENT

Etta Dachman

I retired almost seventeen years ago
The years very quickly did flow
I spent much time with my grandchildren
That time will never be forgotten.
I took many trips
Some by planes and some by ships.
I learned to play the recorder
From more than one instructor.
I tried my hand at oil painting
Needlepoint, crocheting and knitting.
I am somewhat computer literate
I have to learn more, I admit.
The greatest achievement was, by far
I learned to drive, to drive a car.

SNOWSTORM

Etta Dachman

When winter takes hold
It gets very cold.
When the north wind blows
It usually snows.
St. Valentine's Day opened with a mix of snow and sleet
It fell on grasses and on concrete.
Here, no roads were closed
However, they were heavily glazed.
They weren't easily plowed
There wasn't any crowd.
Snow fell mostly at the beginning and at the end of the storm
This was not the norm.
Many couples were forced to cancel supper by candlelight
That made them lose their appetite.
Bouquets of flowers were not delivered
The ice and traffic made them shiver.

THANKSGIVING

Etta Dachman

Thanksgiving is a day for a feast
With many guests at least
Relatives and friends come from afar
By plane and by car.
There is laughter and gaiety
And so much hospitality
The camaraderie of a family gathering
Where everyone is chattering.
The turkey is delicious – so tasty
What a wonderful party
The side dishes are variable
All displayed on a big table.
I am grateful to be born in the U.S.A.
I give thanks on every Thanksgiving Day.
Thanksgiving is a time to share
And to think of everyone for whom you care.

TRAVEL

Etta Dachman

I have traveled far
By plane, boat and car.
I've been to many states
On many different dates
I've traveled to neighbors in the north
I visited others in the south.
I enjoyed islands in the Caribbean
And far off places in the Mediterranean
I've been to Europe often
To places never to be forgotten,
To Israel in the Mid-East
To see many sights at least.
In Asia, I loved Japan
Which I found to be spic and span.
My last trips were to China
To Hong Kong and the Yangtze River.
Some places I did not see
Going there was too risky.
Now I am without a mate
I am a little more sedate
I am satisfied with trips for the day
With senior Centers, I go to see a play.

Stephen Gold

In his youth, Stephen wrote songs, parodies and a column for a young adults' group paper. The column was entitled *Steve's Corner*. He eventually became the editor. He wrote his first poem five years ago. His mother, Ida Gold (1923-1998) was very caring and compassionate. She was a loving mother of two, grandmother of three, and was well-read. She wrote mostly journals and articles on current events. She was also my inspiration.

A JEWISH MOM

Stephen Gold

I will never forget my mom, Ida Gold
Against social injustice, she was very bold.
Ida, wasn't a quitter; she was a real fighter
A woman who had tremendous artistic abilities.
An exciting poet, an insightful artist, and a writer inside her
There was a lot of joy, compassion, and love
She is a woman no one will ever forget
To her, we will always be in great debt
Ida was a great mother to Mary and Steve
A mother in law to Helen, who was more like a mother
Which was very hard to believe.
A wonderful grandma to Susan, Ryan and Andy
They will never forget this amazing granny
It's not only Ida's family who will never forget her
It's everyone who ever met her.
Ida was proud of being a Jew;
Her Jewish history was not a mystery,
When we think of Ida, we sometimes weep and sometimes smile;
She was a mother, grandmother and activist
Who always went the extra mile
My mom, Ida, will live forever in our hearts and mind
She definitely was one of a kind.
To chocolate, she had a serious addiction
A person who read, a lot about facts and fiction
Truly a woman of firm conviction.
Her death certificate said years ago she did depart
But Ida, the fighter, will be alive in every heart
Of every person she ever helped or knew
The memory of Ida, will be eternal
She will always be beside us and guide us
Her love will always shine in our memories.

A WORLD IS BORN
UNDER YOUR FOOT STEPS

Stephen Gold

We are on the beach with young children walking;
There are many birds flying and squawking.
These kids are innocent and fearless, too
They don't yet comprehend this world of stress and demand.
All they see is sun, sea, and sand
It seems like the world out of their footsteps was born
Bare footed, not afraid of stepping on a thorn.
Young and excited by everything,
Each day, there is a new song to sing.
I remember very clearly, and now I see,
Years ago, one of those kids was me!

CHARLES

Stephen Gold

A man who was an inspiration
To Mosholu Senior Center for many years
Charles was an interesting poet, and a leader with much dedication
He was a man who stood up for what he believed
Charles was a very compassionate person
President of the Advisory Board, Harmony Club, and Social Action
His poems encouraged us, made us laugh, and cry
He fought the crooked politicians in the Social Action Group
He was a great leader of the Harmony Club
This wonderful personality, we will never forget
"He was an ordinary person, who did extraordinary things"
(This was Charles' favorite quote.)
Even when Charles struggled with his health
He continued to be there for the people of the center
We won't remember the man who was sick and frail
We will always remember Charles as a vibrant leader,
A poet and fighter who never failed
A man of compassion, and love
For the people in the Senior Center
Tears will be shed for this wonderful man
Charles will live forever in our thoughts, hearts, and mind
I have to say he was one of a kind
His life was filled with love for all.

DAILY NEWS

Stephen Gold

Fires, murders, child abuse
Bad news what's the use?
Drunken drivers, corrupt politicians
Going to war that should not have been
Many deaths, a horrendous scene
The front page story that should be in the back
Scam artists galore, people losing more, and more
Drugs, perverts and sexual harassment
Lot of trouble in our government
Which is in disarray
Sports, movies, and the Stock Market
Most of the news is sad, and bad
Not too much will make you glad
Everything in the papers is always the same
Isn't that a shame?

FRANK

Stephen Gold

My life is more exciting and different now
Because my daughter gave birth
To a beautiful baby, boy.
A gift from heaven, a bundle of joy,
He's cute, alert and energetic.
I'm fascinated by his handsome charm
It is so great to hold him in my arms.
I looked at other grandchildren,
And I wanted one of mine
Now the feeling is definitely divine.
I'm very proud to say that Frankie is my grandson
I show his pictures to everyone
So the world around me can see
What God helped my daughter and my
son-in-law to give me
I want to be there
To see him physically grow and mentally expand,
To always love him and hold his hand
Being a grandfather is really grand!

HELEN, MY QUEEN

Stephen Gold

A woman who is a great inspiration
A wife, a mother who compares to no other
She never had a sister or a brother
Her father was a wonderful man
Who taught her great things about living a better life.
She was taught how to deal with stress and strife
That's why now she is very strong.
I fell in love with this wonderful gal
She became my confidant, wife, and pal
For our married life of forty-four years
Which turned out to have much joy and many tears.
At times it was a struggle but it was worth it
When we began to snuggle.
She was always there when I was in need
She planted an inspirational seed
She was organized you see, but not me
She was good with money and paying the bills.
Helen, helped me through a tough mental condition
It took a lot out of her and our daughter
But without them I couldn't have made it.
A mother who helped our kids learn about life
They stayed out of drugs and all other evils of this life's scene
She is the best wife
One that I could never do without
Of this there is no doubt.

HOW MANY WAYS DO I THANK THEE

Stephen Gold
(This poem was written by Ida Gold, Stephen's deceased mother)

"How many ways can I thank thee, Helen, daughter of mine

for thy loving care throughout the years sharing joys and

sorrows, reaching with outstretched arms and warm heart,

to laugh and weep in times of beauty and grief in the still of

night, memories come floating by

to count how many ways

I can thank thee."

ON VALENTINES DAY

Stephen Gold

On Valentines Day, it is not what you say,
It is what you feel in your heart.
Love is not just an empty emotion;
It is all of your loving devotion
Love is kind, love is pure,
When you both decide to endure (until the end)
Love is having a best friend;
Love is laughing together and crying with each other
Love is giving more than just receiving
Love is compromise, not just one side
Love is truthful; not deceiving
Love is something in which you will abide,
Love is a journey, not just a ride
Love is sincerity, and mostly, it's caring
Love is something that will last if you are always sharing
Love is knowing, love is showing, love is growing.
Love is gratefulness and faithfulness
Love is not just me, but it's also you
Love is your heart entwined in mine
Love is something that can be divine
Love is something that will last,
If you don't always dwell on the past.
True love is something for which you should always pray,
And not only think about it on Valentine's Day
Be sincere, be in love the whole year
"Love is a two way street where neither will ever get lost and over the
Years the most precious gift at any cost."

PREJUDICE OR GOD'S LOVE

Stephen God

Racism and prejudice come from an ignorant mind,
Hatred, anger and bitterness has made them blind,
Because they don't fully understand that God made them equal,
With his love and powerful hand.

Prejudice is taught to us when we're very young,
By parents and teachers who use half a brain,
When dealing with children they want to train.

If you take children of different colors, nationalities or backgrounds,
You'll never have an argument about each other
They won't make a single sound.

So let us try to do something about this horrible mess –
By teaching adults and children to be blessed
By God's love and guidance
So they won't be prejudiced and emotionally stressed.

RED

Stephen Gold

Red is a heart on a Valentine
Red is blood that's in your body
Red is a sunset that is really fine
It's also the color of a dress
The color of the hair of a girl and boy
Red can be the color of your pet
Red is the color of communism
It's also a rug or a bookcase
When you're mad you see red
Red is one of the colors of a traffic light
Red is part of the American's Flag
Red is good red is bad
Red is happy red is sad.

THE WINTER OLYMPICS

Stephen Gold

A beautiful snowy scene in sunny Italy:
Skiers flying down a mountainside
Speed skaters racing for top prize
Win a medal for country, and for self.
Give it all you got, whether you win or not
Be satisfied with your results.
Hockey players playing with reckless abandon
Feeling sore when on their butts, they're land 'n
Its not just about medals and pride,
It's about good sportsmanship
About international competition,
With unity and love.
These fit together, just like a glove.

THE CONTRAST OF WINTER

Stephen Gold

Winter is here with its holiday cheer
A beautiful picture
Of snow covered houses, streets and trees.
Then comes the icy blast of a breeze
It's the end of the lovely winter scene
Now it starts to get very mean
A blizzard and storms with ice on the ground
Knock you off your feet
This is not a sweet treat
Despite this awful wintry blast,
We think of happy winters of our childhood past
Snowballs, sleds and with mittens tied together
In this frozen weather.
We don't want to come in when Mommy does call,
Because we are all having a ball
Then come the chills,
With colds and the flu, then the doctor's shots,
So much suffering from all of our ills
Then we are glad that it's over
Soon it will be Spring
We will see the grass and hear the birds sing
Because Spring is in the air
"Play ball, kids." Baseball players play
Baseball everywhere.

THE STORY OF PRECIOUS GOLD

Stephen Gold

We have a pussycat and "*Precious Gold*" is her name
She is very nosy into this and that
Doing what she wants is the name of her game
She is an interior decorator
Who puts her feeding bowl all over the place
Spilling water, which is a big disgrace
We still love that precious pussycat, even though
She sometimes acts like a spoiled brat
She tries to dominate and run the house
She's lived with us for fourteen years;
If we ever lost her, we would all be in tears
Her actions make us all crazy,
She's some times energetic and some times lazy
Hours before breakfast, she walks across the bed
Precious, makes an effort to stomp on our head
Trying to tell us she wants to be fed.
She climbs in the sink
Trying to get herself a drink
She gets her way
Every minute of every day
When I get mad and yell at her
She climbs on my lap, so I can pet her,
And then, she begins to purr.
On my clothes, she sheds a lot of fur
This is my story of *Precious Gold,*
A cat who's lovable and mighty bold.

THE TRIPLE CROWN

Stephen Gold

First, there was the Kentucky Derby
Run on an off track
The favored horse was Smarty Jones.
He figured to win his seventh in a row
The horse was undefeated
Could he possibly be unseated?
In this race was a horse;
With early speed, named Lion Heart
Could he last until the end?
This horse was really on fire;
He jumped to the lead
Would he accomplish the deed
Of stopping Smarty Jones?
The two horses headed for home
Lion Heart was still in front,
And then came Smarty,
Who was now in second place
To challenge, and win the race.

On to The Preakness, at Pimlico,
Smarty tried to win eight in a row
At the end, instead of a mad scramble,
The race was a runaway and a shamble.

On to the Belmont Triple Crown
It hasn't been done since 1978.
A horse named Affirmed
Was the Triple Crown winner
If Smarty could win it
He would really be great.
What will happen in the Belmont Stakes?
Will it be a Smarty party,
Or a disappointing upset?
What's your idea or your bet?
Here we are on June 5, 2004 Saturday,
For the Triple Crown,
Will this be a special day?
Last year was Funny Cide
Trying for a winning ride
To win the Triple Crown
But the horse didn't win; it went down
This time, in Belmont, was great expectation
For every one in Philly and in New York
Also, in the rest of the nation
Smarty started the race looking swell
It looked like he would ring the bell.

When he went to the lead, it really looked great
Like he would accomplish this deed.
Royal Assault and Bird Stone came in fast
Would Smarty now make his move?
Would he erase the failures of the past?
Were the other jockeys ganging up on Smarty
To spoil his party?
Bird Stone moved in to challenge Smarty Jones
About this, there were no bones,
For the second year in a row,
Would fate rear it's ugly head and say no?
The horses were in the stretch, and heading for home
Now we're coming to the end of this poem.
The "Philly Flash" wanted the cash,
But the big underdog named Bird Stone
Said, "Wait a minute, hold the phone."
This is not a sure thing for the favored horse
"I'm going to win this race."
Bird Stone shot past by Smarty, like he was standing still
For the trainer, and for the fans, this was a bitter pill.
We waited 26 years for a Triple Crown winner;
But as Bird Stone crossed the finish line
Ahead of Smarty, another big disappointment
"Smarty Jones let us down."
After twenty-six years, another time of many tears,
When we thought there would be great cheers.
We have to wait many a year for a Triple Crown winner.

TRACY ROBINSON

Stephen Gold

We love you Tracy with all our hearts
We 're very sad that you had to depart
You've been here for us for many years
Through all of the laughter and all the tears
We have sweet memories of memory lane
You made Trivia a really fun game.
Bingo, without you, will never be the same
When personal problems plagued us
You were there with answers most of the time
When we went on trips to interesting places
Like Woodlock Pines, you put smiles on our faces
When we needed encouragement or someone to help in our clubs
We knew you would come through.
I don't know how we will ever replace you;
You have shown care and concern for us
Now we want to reciprocate;
We will never forget all you have done
How our hearts you have won;
Our families just like a son
Our hope for you is health,
Happiness and success in a new job.

Florence Mendel

Was born in her parents' home in the East Bronx, New York. When her three children became teen-agers, she was accepted in a Special Baccalaureate Program at Brooklyn College. She received her Masters in Rehabilitation Counseling from NYU. Her family have enthusiastically encouraged her writing of poetry.

30,000 CHILDREN

Florence Mendel

I just heard that 30,000 children
Worldwide, die each day of hunger-related causes.
What a tragedy to contemplate!
It gives us something to think about and pause.

To figure out what could be done to alleviate
This condition of world neglect of our future generations,
We have so much here, and much to spare
There must be a way to show we care
About 30,000 children who die each day
Of hunger related causes.

A ROMANTIC INTERLUDE

Florence Mendel

She entered the car to romantic music
How lovely she thought, and hugged and kissed him!
He put his arms around her, and she did the same
Thus engaged in the moment, when the music stopped!
The weatherman broke in to explain
She became distracted and exclaimed,
"What is he saying? Is it going to rain?"

AH, SPRING!

Florence Mandel

Does it have a lovely ring?
Flowers bloom, birds that sing?
Well, that may be for some,
But not for me – I'm not dumb.
It is allergy time (it all flows)
Hacking cough, itchy eyes, runny nose.
Budding trees, grassy green
Not for me; it's a nightmare dream.
Waiting for those clear, warm days
With no pollen around, just the sun's rays.

CROWDS

Florence Mendel

I cannot be one in a crowd
Feeling hemmed in, breathing hard and loud
Pushing, shoving, panic sets in
I try my best to stay within
The boundaries of the crowd;
But I need the air, the space to move about
This is my persona, without a doubt,
No crowds for me!

EVERY DAY IS A GIFT

Florence Mendel

Every day is a gift
Feel the love
The worth of each.

Everyday is a gift
Give some happiness
It is always fit.

Every day is a gift
Look around you
Experience the wonder.

Every day is a gift
Why stress and fume;
Only to get in a snit.

Every day is a gift
Accept it graciously
Time is short.

FOR FLORENCE

Florence Mendel
(The author of this poem is Mary Jones, deceased on April 2007)

"For Florence, friend of many busy years
I thought to write a tribute in a style
She studies now, and not without some fears.
I bravely set about to make her smile.

She brings such glee to learning that it seems
Her age is quite forgotten; years don't count.
Her mind is rich with memories and dreams
Of better worlds where all will share 'The Fount.'

My friend was once a worker, union proud,
And then a wife; her sailor far away.
At last in peacetime, motherhood allowed
Her passing years to fly and joy to stay.

Now, Florence, reads and thinks and learns
And share the gifts her lively spirit earns."

GREAT GRANDMA SPEAKING

Florence Mendel

We are four generations in our family
How lucky can we be?

Adorable Devon – almost two
Interested in everything – old and new.

Learning new words, especially "No".
Testing the waters, challenging Mom and Dad
With a mind of his own. He is quite a lad.

But Great Grandma (that is me)
Just loves him, no end
He is smiling, hugging,
Exploring the trends.

INVITATION

Florence Mendel

People say, "Spring is just around the corner".
Time to take stock in one's self.
Have you noticed the days are getting longer?
Shed some clothes, lose some weight, feel well.
Allow the breeze to make you tingle.
Time is now, can't you tell?
Enjoy the moment, let it mingle
Weave a spell –
Bounce, stretch, jump and sing.
Smell the flowers; renew your spirit.
It has arrived; another spring
So come along, and get with it.

OPEN HEART SURGERY

Florence Mendel

"It's as good as it gets"
Is what the surgeon said
I waited with Steve to see
How the surgery came out.
The tension is over; I sigh with relief
I smile, but don't quite shout.
In the I.C.U., we look at Ted
He is asleep with tubes in his head.
"It's as good as it gets"
Is what the surgeon said!

RECUPERATION

Florence Mendel

Well, it is good to be back
When life is a sad song
And you are away too long.

It is great to be back,
Missed you folks, that is no flack
Seeing the familiar faces,
Discussing issues, touching bases.

Happy to be back,
And that's a fact.
Halleluyah!

RED

Florence Mendel

Red: A multifunctional color
Do we know what for?

Dialysis: Red-blood cleaning
To improve the condition: better feeling

Little Red-riding hood looked and saw
The big bad wolf's gleaming jaw

A Red flag means danger
Watch out, look about!

The Red carton of Silk Soymilk
A good drink to have without guilt

The Cincinnati Reds now seem
To be an okay ball team

A Red ball of fire on high
In a summer-sunset sky

The Red flag of labor
Fighting conditions of favor

Red cheeks abound
In winter's cold sound

The lady in Red –
The "fellas" are crazy
About the lady in Red

I see a Red Exit sign,
"Adieu, So-long, Good-bye."

SEASONS

Florence Mendel

I love the four seasons:
Winter, summer, autumn, spring
They more or less keep their reasons
For what they bring:
Brisk air of winter
Early stirrings of spring
Delicious warmth of summer
Colors of autumn sing.
Lucky us to have the seasons
Live each with zest and reason.

THE DILEMMA

Florence Mendel

I will be going overseas –
It is no time to get married
Wait till I return,
And victory is firm.

I can make some quick plans
With family and friends.
We love each other; no time to wait
Until the war ends.
Even apart, our marriage will endure
We will write each day; of that I am sure.

Suppose we become engaged
By this bonding, all will know
Of our lasting love.

What a wonderful suggestion!
We can start the party plans,
Invite all without question.

THE OCTOGENARIAN WAY

Florence Mendel

On becoming 80 years old
One must be careful (I am told)
About what you eat and what you do.
"Slow down, take it easy" Is that true?

Well, strangely enough,
I do not feel like a powder puff,
Aches and pains take a back seat
When a day turns out really sweet.

I do not know what is in store
I deal with what comes up; there is more –
Live each day "Expectantly."
With friends and family, happily
This is the octogenarian way.

THESE HANDS

Florence Mendel

These hands thrill me at his touch
Every day I look forward to the time
When lightness of being from his touch
Makes me rise, meet hands
That mean so much in my life.
Titillating!
Exhilarating!
Lovemaking!

TRAVEL URGE

Florence Mendel

Though we traveled when our health was good,
Our children are grown,
We have not been anywhere of late.
The challenge now is where to go
For 80-year olds, that accommodates and excites the senses
Ah ha! "Elder Hostel" holds out promise
Of learning, while traveling.

We are ready to make some choices
Will keep you informed as to where and when
The offerings are boundless,
The price is right –
Here we go for a new adventure,
Out of sight!

WINTER IN THE BRONX

Florence Mendel

So far, so good I say
But, who knows what's down the road
Do your best – take each day
And enjoy, though it's cold
Through rain, snow and ice
Keep warm, cath up on chores
Te van will take you (nice)
To the Center to see friends
Life goes on – so savor
What's around till winter ends.

YEARLY CHECKUP

Florence Mendel

Going to the dentist for a cleaning
(I do have an intermittent toothache)
Could it be more?
Next is the eye doctor
(I see moving black dots)
What does it mean?

Hearx follows; review my hearing
(I can't hear as well as I used to)
Do my hearing aids need adjusting?

My mammo is due
(some anxiety here)
Negative! I sigh with relief

Hurrah! All systems are good!
Full steam ahead!
Another year under my belt!

THINK PINK

Florence Mendel

Think pink
It is cherry and happy
A lovely high
Look at the sunset glow
In a Pink sky

Pink is a good-feeling thing
Makes me feel light, airy
Like a bird on the wing

I want to keep this "Pink" feeling
As much as I can
Sometimes it gets me reeling
Pink, Pink, Pink, WHAM!

Flordelisa Mota

Was born in Santo Domingo, Dominican Republic. She lives with her husband Alejandro, in New York City. Mota graduated from Hunter College with a BFA in Creative Writing. Her collection, *Poems of Nature* was published by Xlibris in 2004. She was the winner in 2005 of *Poets in New York*, and won over many competitors the right to be published in *Olive Tree Mythology*. She is the daughter of the Dominican poet Ramón Guzmán, who was imprisoned and tortured twelve times by the Dictator Trujillo's regime, for advocating freedom of speech in the Dominican Republic. Mota has traveled throughout Central and South America, as a Missionary, working with children. She currently works in Hunter College as a tutor of creative writing. She teaches ESL students in the International Center in New York City. Her hobbies are cooking and gardening at the Bronx Botanical Garden.

ARIZONA SOIL

Flordelisa Mota

He returns from Iraq
Joy and pain his smile;
Myrrh – the bitterness of a brutal war,
And honey the sweetness of returning to America,
His native land.
At the airport he kneels and kisses the ground
As no Pope has done before.

It takes him four years to get back home
With tales about the war for everyone to hear
Because the Stars and Stripes Banner never left his heart.

He had experienced hostilities
enough to blow anyone's mind.
In Surprise, Arizona,
Forty-five minutes Northwest
Of downtown Phoenix, where he arrives,
music, bands, balloons blue, white and red,
were not there to greeting him.

He was one more veteran;
Frankincense for his hot town
And that was all.

GREEN MAGNETS

Flordelisa Mota
(To Fanny, Barbara's Loving cat)

Vivid emeralds
they are like an illusion
that trespassed my consciousness

Rays of green light
looking feverishly
for your half soul

Your eye contact
kept looking
beyond human's perspective

How quiet are the expression of your gaze
tranquil as a lake
undisturbed by greed

You could not pronounce
my name
but the magnetism of your sight
followed at the times.

We are bonded together
your closeness
warm the chill
of human's indifference

You felt affection for me
and in the whole world
you loved me the most

Many lives had passed
before I met you
your destiny was to give me love
mine – to adore you.

THE TENTH MUSE

Flordelisa Mota

White eyelashes
Moving up and down
As a silk Chinese fan

You cover his eyes
So I cannot see his soul
Mischievous pieces of Amber
Cruel and kind at once

You have been kissed
By Mnemosyne and Zeus daughters;
Nine goddesses' lips
But none of them loves you
As me

Because I am a Muse
Without a face –
He cannot kiss me back.

H $_2$ O

Flordelisa Mota

Frozen ice
On the side-walk
On top of roof
Porch and cars

You are the trees nightmare
Fear by the fragile
Avoid by the elders

When the sun kisses you
Your soul hard and cold
Will melt
As tears of a Magdalene

Water appears on the surfaces
Cleansing the streets
What a sight! Impurities disappears

The nature of humans is to be wicked
That is why the water – will freeze again.

MARRIAGE

Flordelisa Mota

The bride is dressed all in white
pearls on her wreath
as drops of tears from the sea – trembles.

Six yards, the length of her veil.
Tulle likes fresh snow spreads from her head.
The white Roses on the aisle shivers.
She feels cold as hail.

The cottage – perfume with wild Lilacs,
Mischievously sleeps with one eye closed;
Accomplices of the iron bed.
Honor and traditions pays respect to one another.

Tomorrow the golden sun
will kiss the young bride
a slave –
his Queen.

MOUNTAIN GOLD

Flordelisa Mota

Carpet of colors
Yellow, red, lime, brown and green
Your beauty expands
Freely as a sweet dream

At the distance
Your leaves
Give the illusion
Of golden coins
Dropping at the command
Of your inner life

Mohawk Mountain
Beauty of Nature
Excitement to the shy
Richness for the poor
Inspiration for poets and dreamers
Paradise lost
Now redeem.

PATTERN OF TIME

Flordelisa Mota

Passing by is the clock of eternity
That never stops

What we passionately love today
Tomorrow we will hate

Who could grasp
That moment of happiness
And erase the scar of distress ?

PRISM

Flordelisa Mota

Rainbow of my dreams
Arc of colors, green, purple, and blue
Majestic in your simplicity.

Colorless drop of rain,
The sun sees
Your loneliness, and kisses you
With the fire of his brightness.

At a gallop on a cloud
I found the hiding place
Of peace
Rainbow of my dreams.

PROMISEE

Flordelisa Mota

"Your love is poison
forbidden by life
let me drink it
from your lips
and die."

In Florence, Italy
A twenty first Century, *Juliet*
whispers to her *Romeo*.

RED LITTLE HOOD

Flordelisa Mota
(This poem was written by Muriel Guishaid)

Under the red hood
It is a beautiful girl
With rosy cheeks
And golden curls
She is going through the woods
With a basketful of food.

Bad Wolf, bad Wolf
Sleeping on Grandma' bed
But a hunter comes in
And kill him.

Never do bad
To the little girl
Under the red hood
Because you never know
A woodman could be looking
And your story would end.

RISEN

Flordelisa Mota

The winter has been left behind
as an old garment patched and out of use.
Pain and sorrow
as a dark cloud disappeared.

The longing of the ground for greenery
has ended
sweet elixir of Maple trees
are up as a cascade of dreams.

Earth is in love with the sun
and in a rapture he made her fecund:
the trees were in full leaves
and a heavy south wind was blowing.

A new loud murmur among the new stems
the spring had come with a rush; the people noticed
the message of life – earth has risen;
winter had been defeated.

In the suburbs, where laborers sat before daybreak
the murmur of the trees sounded louder;
they were amazed to see them
waiting for someone
to buy their services at a bargain.

SALTY LIPS

Flordelisa Mota

How many lies
Are hidden
Behind your white teeth

You are the first male
I met with red lips
Pomegranate are they
From Eros' feast

What a surprise
To taste them salty
Instead of sweet.

SALUTE

Flordelisa Mota

At last –
the march ended
and the wearied one shall rest
strained soldiers finally
found a place to break.

At the distant, triumphant,
the Striped Spangled Banner
victoriously kissed the wind
saluting the Platoon fifty one
happily waved.

SILENCE

Flordelisa Mota

The roar of a big city
Is intense
With so many noises, shouting, and outcries
Still each sound has a particular wave.

The honk of an impatient taxi driver
Who put his life at risk
Competing with the hammer
Of a worker in the pavement of a street
Men's voices in base, alto, and tenor
Discussing Base Ball games
All in disarray
Scattered in the air.

Airplanes, steel birds
With lifeless stiff wings
Imposing their way in the sky
Defeating the almighty gravity
With a noise of temporary triumph.

Ambulance and police's sirens
In a dissonant duet
Made the fire engine blush
On the way to stop death.

A blind young man, with a skinny stick
Was happily singing the song *Peace*
As a promise for a better tomorrow
Regardless of the noise
That song I heard.

THE LIGHTHOUSE OF PHAROS

Flordelisa Mota

It was late in the afternoon
The sun lazily was leaving with his light
Embracing her with his golden illumination
And kissed her with the heat if his passion
Constantly every sunny day; since the house was built

The lighthouse told him that she was tired
And would like to travel, leaving behind the sea.
Her staying has been for too long
Warning travelers
That below destruction sleeps.

She has been the friend of sailors
Who looked anxious to her radiant face
In the mist of obscurity.
"I was born in the year two hundred B.C.
I have been here since then.
My longing is to be on another place
Far from this shore and the ripple of the sea.
The constant beats of the waves
And the strong winds from the North
Did not extinguish my light.
I defeated all my opponents; but now I'm tired of this vigil
I would like to live in another place,
To see the frivolous excitement of Alexandria."

The sun said, "Around you are dangerous rocks and reefs.
You are the adorable sight the navigator looks for
Your nature is to guide and save precious lives from disaster."

"Others will take my place.
I am calling earth, my natural ally,
To help me –
I tell her everything and as a good mother
Listen to my plea."

It was felt a tremor
In the whole island of Pharos
The basement of the lighthouse moved
And the six hundred feet of marvel shivered
Projecting the light out to freedom.
It was the year 1375 A.D
But for the shining prisoner – now free
The event happens today.

THE PALACE

Flordelisa Mota

She has arranged her chamber
With red velvet and trimming of gold
Her bed has Jasmine and roses
Above the bin made of sandalwood
Spread scent of life

Her beloved is coming
A hero, with the flag of commitment
At his side.
He promised to return
When the Magnolias bloom

When he appeared
The early dew has dried
Still under his eyelashes
Two dancing drops shine

"I have been waiting for you,
Since the beginning of time
Each beat of my heart told me
That you were near"
She said
"I was building a palace for you
Close to the clouds
Higher than the eternal
Mountains of Tibet"
He responded

.

The song of the birds stopped
They liked to listen
"Come my love with me,
To the palace clear as crystal
With nine doors
Made of jasper stones
On top of each one
With emeralds engraved
Is your name

Lets go to my palace made of dreams
Where Roses, Gardenias, Begonias and Lilies
Al year around are reborn
Tomorrow the light of dawn will take us far
And *Endless Love* will be
My epic poem to you."

WHITE SAVANNA

Flordelisa Mota

A hunter from the North
came like an apparition
covered with fresh snow;
it was a clear day
yet there seemed
an intangible fade over the sled,
a gloom that made the dogs trot
mysteriously as life under the frozen lake.
The aurora borealis
flamed coldly overhead.
The stars, leaping on the frost
madly in love with ice danced
and the land, numb and frozen
under its pall of snow, shivered.

The grey furs of the huskies dogs
made a lapping sound
and they jogged refusing to be frozen
because they sense life not far away
their song was pitched
in minor key with long drawn wailing
and half sobs; it was more than a pleading for life.
The traveler's black beard
and mustache were frosted
as a touch of time
had left an indelible mark on them.

He arrived at a cabin
with the last strength of life
frozen, tired, his brown eyes glittering from the deep cold.
He entered as a stranger
but when night come down
his dogs would be fed
because he possesses
the warmth of faith – in his soul.

ABUSE

Flordelisa Mota
(This poem was written by Madeline Chiciacos)

The girl is only seven years old
The cold chills of fear,
Pain and hunger run through her bones

She crouches into the corner of the kitchen
Not wanting to feel the pain of the belt
Against her torn flesh
From her little body, the energy has gone

Her eyes could hardly be opened
Still, on a rocking chair
She rocks back and forth
Wondering how her mother could be so cruel

She clinches onto useless piece of a paper cup
Looking for love
As the rain continues to fall.

Jorge Rivera

He was born in Puerto Rico and raised in the South Bronx. His father was a struggling merchant and in 1948 immigrated to the U.S. in search of better opportunities. Rivera has three grown children, one is a schoolteacher, and the youngest attends college. Rivera attended RCA Technical Institute. In 1961, he entered the U.S. Navy, specializing in Communications. He saw action aboard the cruiser, U.S. Newport News, part of the flotilla that circled the blockaded Cuba for twenty days in 1961. He was honorably discharged as a Petty Officer Second Class in 1964. He is now retired, but continues to be active in his community. He once served as Auxiliary Police Officer in the Bronx 52 Precinct. He is currently a member of the Mosholu-Montefiore Senior Center, and serves on its Advisory Board, and Chairs the Social Action Committee.

CHARLES FRIEDMAN

Jorge Rivera

Charles Friedman, was a kind and gentle soul
Who never saw a need to raise his voice.
But his influence was felt nevertheless
In the halls of this terrific, Mosholu Senior Center.

His only mission in life was to help his fellow man
And in that endeavor he partook in all our activities.
Always inquiring about my Teen daughter and my Mom
He often times rebuked me, but was generous with his praise.

Because I was his Junior, I listened to his counsel
And he always lit up when I mentioned Babe Ruth,
Joe DiMaggio, Phil Rizzuto and Mickey Mantle.
In the corridors of this marvelous Center
His image and memory will be present forever.

HELEN STARKMAN

Jorge Rivera

Helen Starkman, was my friend
Oh, what a wonderful smile she had!
A perpetual smile
Innocent as a child.
Yes, I knew Helen Starkman.

Oh, but Helen also had a temper!
Luckily, she spared me on that count.
I knew better than to antagonize Helen
For she will be forever,
The wonderful lady with the perpetual smile.

MOM AND POP

Jorge Rivera

Mom and Pop were country people, born in Puerto Rico.
She married at 17, had 5 children, and, oh yes, twins on
Christmas Eve. It was tough going with Pop, but toughed
it out, Mom did. War at first sight! Can't recall a compromise;
always black and white. They were true warriors. She finally
dumped Pop, and looked askance at men.

Mom and Pop were truly loved, but also feared. Transgressions
were dealt with swiftly; a declaration of war. On this issue, they
saw eye-to-eye, gender aside. Parenting is tough, but they made
the grade, their way.

Pop bid goodbye at 95, and Mom is still a crackerjack at 90.
Feisty as ever, she still curses Pop. She never wanted to live
too long anyway, but now she is reaching for the stars.
And what would Pop be saying, now?

RETIREMENT

Jorge Rivera

I never thought retirement would come to this:
My old boss would marvel at my production.
Unable to stand still, while the clock goes tick, tick.
Darn it, I'm running out of time, again!

Thanks to good fortune, fitness, and God, I run circles
'round the others. But remember, I am still a junior in the
eyes of my "sistas and brothas."

I'm also awash with mundane activities, and since Charles'
departure, Social Action is my prime duty. Our Drama
teacher is just superb, and the Poetry one, is simply out
of this world!

The Support Group gals are just grand, but the Advisory
Board sessions also merit consideration.

I am also a junky for good and bad news, disdain TV and,
yes, I duly surf the web. But my main throwback is to chat
and to rap with the pack.

I don't know what God has in store for me, but whatever
it is, He has to hurry to catch up with me.

ROAD RAGE

Jorge Rivera

Motorists now-a-days are truly rude and inconsiderate.
Why! They shoot by you like bullets, honking incessantly.
Seniors are particularly vulnerable, since they lack wings
to fly. If they' are lucky, they'll make it across in a cloud of
dust and a short prayer.

Road rage and hit and runs have snowballed and
are a pedestrian's nightmare; and when the authorities
smell a lead, the rascals have simply vanished in mid air.

I, for one, insists that these creatures be snared, not spared,
and if not hanged, banned; or re-settled to a far away land,
like Mars. But, would the Martians want them?

ROSA

Jorge Rivera

We are constantly at her side; her
withering body, slim and spent, not
unlike a twig. Such elegant features
and calm demeanor, masking her pain.

She is a reflection of our Teen daughter,
totally inseparable. Other people's lives
can seem empty and hollow, but not hers.
Despite her torment, she will not leave this
world and is animated at her daughter's sight.

Pain? What pain! Where's my baby?

A mother's love is eternal and unconditional –
to the very end.

THE SWEEP

Jorge Rivera

In the mid-term elections, the incumbents did not hold sway
for leaving the Republic, in disarray. Katrina, Iraq, the scandals,
and Tom Delay, now all come into play. They governed without
a vision, incompetence, illusion and division.

America welcomes the new Speaker of the House, and it is a
woman. Holly Cow! The House and Senate were upended and
the White House, lame duck rendered. The President now has a
new weapon, and it is the Veto pen, Veto pen, Veto pen, Veto pen!

The troops must be brought home rather quickly, otherwise
the Congress will be forced to act, by refusing to fund
this folly in Iraq. Social Security and Medicare were the prime targets
of this President, but the people responded: "Not so fast, Mr. Prez!"

The next election is only two years away, and the sweep is likely to
be completed. The electorate is now bent on kicking the rascals out,
until they are totally depleted and defeated. Clearly, the nation is
demanding change, unity, competency, and vision.

THE FIASCO

Jorge Rivera

The old Vet could not help but cringe
At news of the mounting casualties
His tolerance growing thin
At the turn of eventualities.

Some out there don't give a damn
At this terrible blunder
Learning nothing of Vietnam
And splitting the country asunder.

The President has set the course
With dogged determination
But the electorate has had its say
In the mid-term elections.

As Saddam will meet his fate
When he reaches the gallows
Et you too Bush, has also faced
The irate voters at the polling gallows.

When that faithful day arrives
And the troops come marching home
We will ensure that leaders strive
To leave foreign lands alone

Rose Smeenk

Was born in New York City, two months premature, and she's been rushing through life ever since. In her youth, she engaged in many sports such as tennis, roller and ice skating, skiing and horseback riding. She loves to keep busy, and so, she paints, writes and plays bridge in her senior years. She also swims at the "Y". She lives alone and does her own housekeeping. Although she suffers the twinges of arthritis and other old-age symptoms, she still remains young at heart.

A TIME OF BUOYANCY

Rose Smeenk

Surging through brittle dry leaves
Out from the barren earth
Blushes of pink, dashes of purple
And baby blues of crocus blossoms
Set the clock for spring's debut

A faint froth of greenery coats the barren branches
Twittering, fluttering birds scatter
Some carry twigs in beaks for nest
In the bushes and trees
Zephyr breezes blow thither and yon
Playfully raising clouds of loose debris

It's time for buoyancy, spirits rise
We walk now erect, no longer bent
Against Winter's chill and youth
Is responding to love of life
And love's expectancy.

AWAKE NATION'S CONSCIENCE

Rose Smeenk

Thousands of people marched
Shouting loudly, throats parched
On Washington, D.C' s Capitol grounds

There were crowds at the U. N.
Also celebrities' speeches – a trend
To fire up consciences, shouting alarms

I, too gave loud voice in this masses' parade
Alas, our protests were a charade
Our country's still at war

More than two years and we're still in Iraq;
Over two thousand soldiers will never come back
When will legions of voices be heard?

BOLERO

Rose Smeenk

A whisper of rhythm, rising in tempo
Repetitive, stirring my senses
Sending chills up my spine
As the bolero beat plays on

With closed eyes, I visualize
The sensuous dancers –
The man dark, persuasive, agile;
The woman seductive – a flame
In scarlet skirts whirling
Gracefully, challenging the man
Twirling around him
Flashing bare shoulders towards him,
Swirling her hips to the music's rhythm

I'm holding my breath
As drum and woodwinds
Grow louder and insistent

My fingers pick up the pace.
My shoulders rise up and down
With the scaling beat
Only my seat restrains me
As I respond to the cadence of Bolero.

CHANGE OF MOOD

Rose Smeenk

A rainy, dreary day
Chills me through and through
Fills my mind with the foreboding
Of shadowy, gloom and doom.

A sudden burst of sunshine
Chases the gray clouds away and
Lifts off my cloak of sadness
And I greet hopefully the day.

FOR WHOM THE BELLS TOLL

Rose Smeenk

Rat-a-tat, rat-a-tat. Boom,boom, boom!
A parade passes by, making excitement zoom
The honor guards wave their banners high,
Everyone salutes – hearts swell with pride
Uniformed troops and their marching bands
Honor comrades dead in foreign lands,
Who formerly marched to these rhythms of war
Then were sent away into real battle's roar
The slow boom of drums – eerie sound of taps;
Memorial salutes and percussion traps
Are the reminders of our fallen dead
Over whom special services are read
In cemeteries; reminders of names and place
Of these wars, heroes lying in their graves, embrace
Are the rewards for lost youth who hoped for more
Than the hole in the ground earned by war.

JULY 4TH

Rose Smeenk

Hooplah! Hurray! Parades passing by
Crowds are cheering! One huge cry!
As the marines, sailors, and soldiers march
There's an exhibit of the Washington arch
Young girls prance, tossing pom-pom
Young boys busily beating their drums
It's a day to remember – our start as a nation;
Also the many who gave their lives' obligation
To perpetuate our liberty and democracy
Freedom from past cruelty from autocracy
It's also a time to remember our heroes
Who lie in cemeteries in nations worldwide
To the sounds of taps, let us pray for peace
To the end of wars – let the frays cease.

LIFE

Rose Smeenk

What is life's real meaning?
Is it really in rebirth?
Is it the new seed's gleaning
Sustenance from Mother Earth?

Is it just man's span of dreaming
Secrets of life until death?
The human time is so fleeting
After the infant draws his first breath.

We who live after the dying
Continue to earn life's worth
In loving, seeking and striving
Through many sorrows and mirth.

From father to son. Mother and daughter –
As "Acorns fall from great oak trees"
Or as star and planet, fish in water –
Is life a rebirth of these?

LOVELY VIEWS

Rose Smeenk

Pink streaks thread the dark sky
Crows stir, make raucous cries
I awaken with a start,
Eyelids reluctantly part.

Outside the street lights grow dim
Highway traffic increases din
The skyline fog disappears;
The Palisades reappear

From my 12th floor window
I see afar and below
Among my many lovely views
Are autumn's startling hues

The trees-red, yellow, bronze
Are shedding their summer gowns
The park's lawns are still green
From above, all looks serene

The sky lightens with a sun ray
Promising a lovely day
I'm awake – feeling life's glow
Glad to be "A-rarin' to go."

POETRY

Rose Smeenk

I cannot sing or carry a tune,
Yet music is my daily boon.
I feel it in my soul –
It makes my life force whole
By writing poetry.

Substitute words for music;
Written not always in rhythm or rhyme.
They bare my heartfelt emotions;
Refine inner sight and sensual delight;
By writing poetry.

A poem encourages fantasy,
Weaves beauty into Nature's tapestry.
The trivial and jovial is conveyed
By writing poetry.

A poem is your instrument
To tingle, please or implement
Inner or outer perceptions;
Stands out with verbal expressions
By writing poetry.

PRAISE

Rose Smeenk

Try to praise beauty in the world
In spring, try to remember
The aroma of roses, lilies and lilacs,
New mown grass lawns.
Praise the budding fruit trees
Feel the rebirth of hope,
Revive youth's expectations
And their romantic thrills.

Cast off chills of old age;
Aching bones and sloth pace
Praise being alert and aware
By remembering musical rhythms
Of concerts and melodies.
Cast off sad moments in the past
Praise the new season's arrival;
The longer days and warmer night
Songs of the mocking bird
Greeting morning's early light
Rise to the new dawning of life.

RED

Rose Smeenk

Carmen swirls –
Flashing her red gown
Ruffles ripple red petals
A wind-blown rose
That flows in
Rhythmic response
To operatic theme.

Carmen teases her lover
With a long-stemmed red rose
Between ruby smiling lips.

He sees red as her body teases
Him into red hot passion,
And with flash of a dagger,
He stabs Carmen!

Her life's blood spreads crimson;
Her carmine gown wetly shines
As the burgundy curtain falls
Hiding her crumpled, red heap.

ROMANCE

Rose Smeenk

A star filled night
The moon shines bright
On the summit of a hill
All round, it is very still
One lonely car is parked there
In it, a couple's silhouette is clear
Their profiles are like on a screen
Clearly seen in dim light's gleam
Merge in a prolonged kiss;
An enactment of loving bliss
Ah, youth, by love entranced
My blood stirs by such romance.

SEPTEMBER 11, 2001

Rose Smeenk

I saw HELL rise up to earth on TV
The 11th of September, a day of infamy;
A day that had begun, calm and bright
Each person in the city was at work or at play
Going about on their own peaceful rounds;
When out of the blue, flying demons astound
Out of the sky, they gave a devilish thrust,
Shattering the twin towers, crushing them to dust

With this vast crash, 3000 occupants met their doom
Into the darkness of a collapsing tomb
Witnesses, helpless, paralyzed with frantic fright
Wept at this treachery and for the victims' plight
Heroes came forth trying to salvage what they could
Some of them lost their lives doing good
Now memorials are erected at Battery Park
As this catastrophe has forever left its mark

Today, we strive for universal harmony
A world at peace, free from treachery.

SILENCE

Rose Smeenk

Where are we when we fall silent?
My ears alert to the slightest sound
The rustle of the wind through the trees above
Distant twittering of a bird's song,
Crackle of leaves under foot, the slough
Of a watery trickle around a stone
Above, clouds moving softly in the sky
The sun's rays glimmer
sparkling dew drops on leaves
Only my heart is heard as a
rhythm to Nature's symphony.

SONNET

Rose Smeenk

I am enjoying the comforts of old age
I feel free, agile and clear of mind
Live from day to day, relish time's new page
New diversions are not hard to find
I raised a family, my life's been full;
Endured love's loss; I have sweet memories
Enjoyed all my travels. Life was not dull.

I can take my ease now fortunately
How long will I last till time takes its toll?
There were dreams in my youth, now I have none
In my old age, what should be my goal?
I think of many things still left undone
Now my memories bring joys of the past
So I write my poems to make them last.

STRIVING FOR ETERNITY

Rose Smeenk

The strivings of most humanity
From earliest days of history
Have been to better man's lot in life
To overcome plodding toil and strife.

The first bone or stone used as a tool
The glittering shell or metal jewel
A bit of clay fashioned into a bowl
Raised the sights of obtainable goal.

Etched images on ancient cave wall
Shows eternally the hunter's role
His art added to his tribe's pleasure –
Now archeological treasure.

Man has reached the moon, traveled in space –
Sung songs and written symphonies of praise
For his great deeds and glorious might
His high instincts have broadened his sight.

The stronger always the weak enslaved
Mass destruction was in hands of the brave
They warred among themselves to great excess
Yet reached for godliness, nothing less.

Churches and prayer satisfied man's soul
Statues, paintings played a cultural role
Trying to transcend life's mortality
He seeks and strives for eternity.

SWAN LAKE

Rose Smeenk

Softly, gracefully, unfolding
Snowy white feathers fluttering
And rising tip-toe to the melody's
Musical strains of Swan Lake.

The "swan's" crown sparkles
As her curving neck bends and flows
With the rhythmic undulating of her arms,
As she seems to float across the stage.

She dips and sways in swan – like majesty.
The spot light enhances the shiny surface
Of her sparkling white plumage
Until she lies again in a downy mound.

TEMPESTUOUS

Rose Smeenk

Can you see the wind?
Sight unseen, you can feel it
through every flap of your coat,
the chill around your neck,
the nip at ears and nose,
frosty fingers and toes.

Leaves scatter and scurry,
branches sway recklessly.
while twigs crackle and break.
Windows rattle, doors creak
dust devil rise and swirl
and flurries of snow sparkle or they fall.

In summer, dulcet breezes hum
while softly stirring leaves and hair;
but winter wind can change its tune
from a soft sigh to a rising roar
to the crescendo of a hurricane
that rips and destroys all in its way.

The wind is tempestuous,
contemptuous in its power,
and all are subject to its many moods.

TIME'S EXPOSURE

Rose Smeenk

Snap – the camera clicks!
Lets in light and sensitivity –
A photographic exposure is made
Of me – frozen in time – young
Clad in my best, standing there;
That photo's in my album now
          For posterity.

No clue to the past here
Nor light upon my future expectations
Nor sensitivity to youthful despairs
The fleeting smile lasts here forever
No reason's given for prideful stance –
Just a pose for my album
          For posterity.

The future of that time is long past.
It's today's present – as I gaze in retrospect
I regret my youth lost to time's exposure
I know my mirror realistically reflects
Those past years have taken their full measure
Time's exposure is now as photo in my album
          For posterity.

UNITED

Rose Smeenk

The day finally came
When in my arms was bestowed
A soft cottony blue cocoon
Unfolded to reveal
Rosy cheeks, puckered lips
Satiny smooth, doll-like face
And tiny sparkling eyes.

For nine months I awaited his appearance.
Now I reveled at this miracle –
His ten, tiny curling finger petals
Ten wriggling round pea-shaped toes
I felt blessed to see his perfection.

I basked in his body warmth against my breast.

Both of us at last united, both of us content in our nest.

Aloha from Hawaii

Dorothy Salvage

Was born in the Bronx, New York City. She started work at seventeen years of age as a full time nurse. She is a graduate of NYU. She raised a family of three children and two grandchildren. She is now retired, loves to travel, and enjoys the Senior Center. Her hobbies include knitting, crocheting and sewing. "Own one cat, but miss my dog," she says.

A LETTER
TO THE POLAR BEARS UP NORTH

Dorothy Salvage

We know you are a marine mammal
Spending most of your life on icebergs.
You are so beautiful; I love you all.
We had 400 years of inventions –
Little did we know what damage, they would do.
Over using, misusing and abusing.
Leading to melting icebergs and pollution.
This turbulence caused by global warming.
We know you are on the front line of this devastation.
I hope, in time, we become more thoughtful about your plight.
We are beginning to hear in the news about this global warming fright.
Perhaps we will save you in time, before you become extinct, over night.

Love, A Fan

MAN IN CAR

Dorothy Salvage

Man, sitting in car, waiting for wife, who is shopping
What is keeping her?
She must be buying out the store
Out she comes with one package
He says, "Women, you can't live with them;
you can't live without them."

GLOBAL WARMING

Dorothy Salvage

Too many clouds to see the sunrise
Too much pollution that blocks the blue skies
The climate is changing before our eyes.
Need I say more; this may be our demise.
The trees turn colors all too soon! Too soon!
Summers are long and hot and too hazy
If you ask me, you should ask a daisy.
Wildlife begs to be spared by the warming
They just know, but they don't know that they know.
We're their keepers; there are many of us
Some one should lead us and spare them the "cuss"
For we all love seeing tigers and bears
And beautiful scenery and fresh air.
Future generations will know we cared.

Dorothy Salvage

Haiku
Barn Yard Noises

Cats Meow – Birds Sing
Pigs Oink – Cows Moo – Horses Neigh
All Noises – O.K.

Winter Scene

Trees – Silver white snow
Santa and his reindeer glow
Daddy's car we tow

Christmas

Christmas Trees we Light
Decorations – Holy Night
Presents wrapped – All Right

My Dog

My Dog – My Back Brace
Is my Hot Water Bottle
Does Keep My Feet Warm.
Van Cortland

LOVE

Dorothy Salvage

Many loves have we automatically,
To name just a few:
"God and country" fathers, mothers, and children
Sisters and brothers, our teachers, best friends and lovers.
All those who serve us in many a way, without a complaint,
By night and by day.
The beauty of the Earth and the four seasons.
The sun, the moon, the stars,
The blue sky that surrounds us.
Don't forget the wildlife.
I melt at the sight of so much diversion,
And the birds in flight.
With all these loves that we are enjoying
We should all be happy and contented.
Last but not least, tools that were invented
To ease our work load, which was intended.

OUR PARKS

Dorothy Salvage

We love our inventions
We have good intentions
But where are our reserves
We're using and abusing
We see this every day
Cars and buses
Trucks and cusses
When is it going to stop?
What can we do to help?
The poles have melted
The tropics have wilted
Soon there will be smog
Let's start anew.
Please spare a few of our parks
So we can have Larks,
And Sparrows and Robins
Eagles and Beagles
Trees and Bees,
Seagulls and wildlife, too.

OUR UNSUNG HEROES

Dorothy Salvage

Let Van Cortland be
    country once again to
City folks such as we
    with the high prices and
Shortages of gas
Van Cortland must be
    like in the past.

We will have country
    right here in the city
If we don't, then,
    Oh What a pity!

For the trees are our soldiers
    I love every leaf –
They make everyone
    want to be
"Commander in Chief."

STOP LOOK LISTEN

Dorothy Salvage

Our animals are talking to us
Loud and clear
The climate is changing
What do we do next year?

I haven't seen a Robin on the wing
I miss the songs they used to sing
Where do they go?
Up to the attic?
They're not used to snow.

The trees turn colors
All too soon
Long before autumn
No full moon,
So we can spoon.

The polar bears are confused
They seem to say,
"Where is the snow?
We used to romp and play."

They claim we are the worst of all the animals
Are we that blind that we cannot see
And feel the warming trend?
What will be happening to you and me
If we don't get our priorities in order?
The tropics or the artic will be in our border.

So listen my children
If you don't take care,
Your planet and yourselves
Will soon disappear.

TRAVELING

Dorothy Salvage

Who loves you, baby?
Even if you lose
Fans do
Who runs a mile between bases?
And even more when you have pain
Muscles aching
Injuries galore;
Most baseball teams do
No use complaining
Even if it's raining
Old golden sun
Ain't no fun
Looking down all day
From 93million miles away
If only he wasn't so strong
Fans are all wrong; I fear
They should all get together and say
"Wait till next year."

VANCORTLANDT

Dorothy Salvage

People don't realize that
Cutting down trees,
Wildlife leaves (birds).

To cut down trees in (N. Y.C) is out of
The question –
When they destroy Van Cortland
There will be too much congestion.
What we need more of
Are Eagles and Hawks
And more birds, people complain
That squawks.

People don't realize for
Every man, woman & child
There are 8-10 rodents,
Rats, mice or ticks.
Take your pick
We should be
In the Army.
Allow me –
Relax; sit back, as you were,
There is too much asthma.

ACKNOWLEDGMENTS

OUR APPRECIATION TO Bayla Lovens, Director of the Mosholu-Montefiore Senior Center, for her support in the early stages of this anthology. Gratitude to Kate Cohen, for introducing me to the poetry class in the Senior Center. Thanks to the Bronx Botanical Garden, where we met, for the magic of their lovely flowers and landscape that continually inspired our metaphors. Thanks to Rose Smeenk, for the beautiful art work on the book cover. I would like to thank Jorge Rivera, for his tireless enthusiasm, and to Steve Gold, for his good counsel in seeing this project through. To Israel Rosario, Computer Science instructor, for his collaboration in typing and in printing many seniors' poems. He was patient and gracious to all. Appreciation to the families and friends of each member of our Friday's poetry class, for their support, love and faith in this book. Thanks to all the seniors members, who make us feel welcome in our second home.

Thanks are also extended to Frank Conte, who edited the complete manuscript.

Flordelisa Mota
Poetry instructor

Printed in the United States
113321LV00006B/412/P